GOLDEN THOUGHTS FROM THE SPIRITUAL GUIDE OF MIGUEL MOLINOS
THE QUIETIST

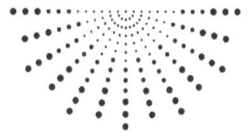

J. HENRY SHORTHOUSE

CONTENTS

LIFE OF MIGUEL MOLINOS.   1
PREFACE.   16

GOLDEN THOUGHTS FROM THE SPIRITUAL GUIDE WHICH DISENTANGLES THE SOUL AND BRINGS IT BY THE INWARD WAY TO THE GETTING OF PERFECT CONTEMPLATION, AND THE RICH TREASURE OF INTERNAL PEACE.

THE FIRST PART. OF THE DARKNESS, DRYNESS, AND TEMPTATIONS, WHEREWITH GOD PURGES SOULS, AND OF INTERNAL RECOLLECTION.   23

THE SECOND PART. OF SPIRITUAL MARTYRDOMS WHEREBY GOD PURGES SOULS: OF CONTEMPLATION INFUSED AND PASSIVE: OF PERFECT RESIGNATION, INWARD HUMILITY, DIVINE WISDOM, TRUE CONCILIATION, AND INTERNAL PEACE.   53

The subjection of human selfishness by holy love, and the subjection of the human will by union with the Divine Will, may be said to make "Christ within us." Christ will come visibly in the clouds of heaven. But in the spiritual sense, He may come now, He may come to-day.

— *MADAME GUYON.*

LIFE OF MIGUEL MOLINOS.

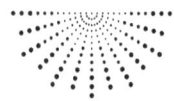

Miguel Molinos, the author of *The Spiritual Guide,* was a cadet of a noble Spanish family of Minozzi, in the diocese of Saragossa, in Aragon. He was born on December 21, 1627, and was educated in Coimbra, where he became a priest and took his theological degree. After much peaceful meditation and long service in the Spanish Church he betook himself to Rome, in order to gain a wider field for the inculcation of favourite doctrines of a mystical theology, which a study of the mediaeval mystics, and the bent of his own pious nature, had induced him to adopt. There, in 1675, he published in Italian his famous little book, which was so soon afterwards translated into Spanish, and won such popularity in his native country that some are still found who declare that the Spanish version is earlier than the Italian. His quietist views had a singular charm for multitudes of earnest, shrinking men and women, who, finding it impossible in that time of fierce warfare and fiercer controversy to get the rest they yearned for in any of the systems of the day, were fain to seek it, like the Stoics during the tumults of the ancient world, or the German mystics during the commotions of the fourteenth century, within the silence of their own souls. He showed them, it seemed to many, how to find *within* the peace denied *without*, either in religious or political companionship. The soul of man, he taught, was the temple and abode of God, and if man's duty was to keep it clean and pure from worldliness and all lusts, his reward was that he could retire within himself and there hold fellowship with God in the temple He had fashioned for Himself.

Molinos taught nothing new, nothing which had not been taught by the mystics of St. Victor, by John Tauler or Henry Suso, by Theresa of Spain or Catherine of Siena. His own holy living, his disinterested piety, and his charm of manner, combined with the reaction against the brawling religion of the day, made his teaching seem to many almost a new revelation, to be received, cherished, and lived on. He became the centre of a great revival of spiritual religion, not only in Rome, but all over Roman Catholic Europe, and, like Meister Eckart in the fourteenth century, had his coteries of praying people whose devotional life he directed by correspondence.

In Rome his circle of friends and disciples included many of the leading nobles and most eminent ecclesiastics, and Pope Innocent XI., who would fain have made him a cardinal, took him, it is said, for some time to be his spiritual director. Bishop Burnet, in his famous letters from Italy, says, "The New Method of Molinos doth so much prevail at Naples that it is believed he hath above 20,000 followers in that city. He hath writ a book which is entitled *Il Guida Spirituale*, which is a short abstract of the Mystical Divinity. The substance of the whole is reduced to this, that, in our prayers and other devotions, the best methods are to retire the mind from all gross images, and so to form an act of faith, and thereby to present ourselves before God, and then to sink into a silence and cessation of new acts, and to let God act upon us, and so to follow His conduct. This way he prefers to the multiplication of many new acts and other forms of devotion, and he makes small account of corporal austerities, and reduces all the exercises of religion to this simplicity of mind. He thinks this is not only to be proposed to such as live in religious houses, but even to secular persons, and by this he hath proposed a great reformation in men's minds and manners. He hath many priests in Italy, but chiefly in Naples, who dispose those who confess themselves to them to follow his methods. The Jesuits have set themselves much against this conduct, as foreseeing it may weaken the empire that. superstition hath over the minds of the people, that it may make religion become a more plain and simple thing, and may also open the door to enthusiasms."

What Bishop Burnet writes is what really happened. The disciples of Molinos became noted for their exemplary lives; they were seen to become more devout, to live retired from the frivolity of the world, and to give themselves over to pious works of charity and brotherly sympathy; but they also were seen to be indifferent to those external ways of manifesting piety which the Romanist Church has always insisted on. They seldom went to mass, they set small store by corporeal austerities, relics, image-worship, and pilgrimages; they spent little upon masses for the souls of deceased relations and friends; and, above all, they neglected the confessional. They did not deny any of the doctrines of the Church, they raised no cry for reformation, they were not tempted to break out into open revolution, and yet they displayed such passive resistance to the whole external machinery of the religious life of the Romanist Church, that had the movement been allowed to go on, the foundations on which the ecclesiastical system of that church rested might have insensibly crumbled away. The movement was a silent revolution, although it displayed no standard of revolt, and the keen eyes of the Jesuits soon discovered its meaning and to what end it was leading.

If God may be met in the silence of the believer's soul, where is there room for the priest, who, according to Romanist ideas, must always stand between the believer and God, and by his act take the hand of faith and lay it in the hand of Omnipotent Love and Power? If penitents do not need to leave their rooms to ask God for pardon and to receive it, what place is there for the confessional, with its profitable money perquisites, and its still more precious secrets? How was the Church, with its court, its cardinals, its army, to be paid and supported, and how could the policy of governments be guided by the priestly *directors* of kings and of queens, of ministers and of generals?

The Jesuits saw that the edifice of Romanism, which they had patiently built up in more inexpugnable fashion than before on the ruins which the Reformation had left, was attacked a second time by a Mysticism not different from that of the fourteenth century, and they dreaded that the second movement might emancipate the Romance nations, as the first had set free the Teutonic.

The whole power, astuteness, and unscrupulousness of the great Order was concentrated in an attack upon "The New Method of Molinos."

Father Paul Segneri, one of the foremost and most popular Jesuit preachers in Italy, was ordered to attack the Quietist principles. The task was a delicate one. If Rome had condemned John Tauler, it had "beatified" Henry Suso; if Margaretta and Christina Ebner, and other pious ladies who had joined the company of the "Friends of God" in the fourteenth century, shared the condemnation of their spiritual leader, Nicholas of Basel, Rome had canonized Theresa of Avila and Catherine of Siena. Since the Reformation the steel hand of Jesuistry had often concealed itself in the velvet glove of Quietism, and the earlier leaders of the Order in Italy owed no small part of their success to the use that they had made of "perishing, languishing tenderness" of the Quietist, St. Francis de Sales.

Father Segneri could not openly attack Quietism. He began by praising the Method but deprecating its use. The Quietist was too good for this world of rude, brawling life, and his Method, however useful to very pious souls, was not fitted for the every-day life of the ordinary Christian. The book, notwithstanding the artistic moderation of the author, raised a storm of opposition, and the sympathy of the ruling powers at Rome was so strongly with Molinos and his followers that when the Inquisition was asked to interfere, and give its judgment, Segneri was condemned, and his treatise, along with some others against Quietism, were put upon the index of prohibited books.

Foiled in this way, the Jesuits tried another. During the latter half of the seventeenth century they furnished many of the favourite confessors and directors of princes, and their influence over Louis XIV. of France was supreme.

As they had made use of Philip II. of Spain and of his descendants on the Spanish throne to send the invincible Armada against England, to attempt to drown the Protestantism of the Netherlands in the blood of its professors, and to set state in array against state in the savageries of that thirty years' war from which Germany has not yet recovered, so in this conflict they made Louis XIV. their instrument for the suppression of a religious revival which was silently sapping the sources of their power.

That king occupied a position in Europe not unlike the place taken by Philip II. in the sixteenth century, and was perhaps more easily moved by ecclesiastical intrigues than the cool fanatic whose plans to crush the Reformation had kept Europe in terror for nearly half a century. He had sins which were dear to him, and he was ready to pay the price which the Jesuits asked for the license they gave him to violate any or all of the commands of the Decalogue. "To be esteemed more Catholic than the Pope, and more fastidious about keeping the purity of the faith than the Holy Office itself, was a reputation worth having for a monarch who was always trying to secure the advantages of religion without any of its privations, and the respect of his subjects without deserving it. Père Lachaise, the King's confessor, made the King believe that nothing he could do would contribute so much to ensure all these results as to bring about the condemnation of Molinos, his disciples, and doctrines. Next to the pleasure of living without any religion himself, Louis XIV. most enjoyed persecuting religion into other people. He yielded to the specious arguments of his wily confessor, and gave orders to Cardinal d'Estrées to denounce Molinos to the Holy Office, and to press his condemnation with the utmost rigour." [1]

The Cardinal d'Estrées had been one of Molinos' strongest supporters, he had sought his confidence and had prided himself on his intimacy with the pious author of *The Spiritual Guide,* but without a moment's hesitation, at the bidding of his royal master, he turned upon his friend and denounced him to the Inquisition. He had even the audacity to say that his friendship with the man he was now clamouring to get condemned had been a pious fraud to discover and unmask the pernicious errors which underlay specious doctrines.

The intervention of Louis XIV., the most powerful Roman Catholic sovereign of the age, so strengthened the cause of the opponents of Molinos, that in 1685 the Inquisition seized him, and imprisoned him to await his trial, and his defenders became panic-stricken. The Inquisition of the sixteenth and seventeenth centuries was a very different organisation from the Holy Office with which the Church of the middle ages had dealt with heresies, real or supposed. The mediaeval Inquisition had been remodelled by Cardinal Caraffa and the Jesuits, and its dread power had stifled the national as well as the religious life of Spain, and had slain all independent thought, active intelligence, and free civic life in Italy. It shrouded itself in secrecy, and struck fiercely whomsoever it threatened. Men feared to confront it.

For long Molinos lay in prison untried. Men said that the Jesuits and the Inquisition waited for the death or the submission of the Pope before openly condemning the theologian whom he had so conspicuously favoured. However that may be, the time was occupied in arresting and examining all who had favoured the Quietist movement, or who had been wont to praise the New Method.

"At length, after twenty-two months' close confinement; after enduring tortures to compel inculpating confessions, of which the world has been permitted to know nothing, except what they are entitled to infer from the well known usages of the Inquisition; after all the letters he had received for more than twenty years had been put into the crucible of their malignity, to extort from them poison that would kill and not betray; after hunting down every man, woman, and child in Rome, not too formidable by their rank or connections, who could be induced by their fears or their hopes to repeat real or imaginary conversations with the accused, Molinos was brought forth from his dungeon to receive the judgment of the Inquisition."[2]

In order to secure a large attendance, an indulgence was promised for fifteen years to all who assisted with their presence at this *Act of Faith,* and the Church of *Santa Maria Sopra Minerva,* the same building in which Galileo, a few years before, had made his recantation with the half audible '*It moves for all that,*' was crowded from floor to ceiling on September 3rd, 1687, to hear the condemnation of the famous teacher, who had been regarded a few years before with almost superstitious veneration as the most pious man in Rome.

An eye-witness, Estiennot, in a letter, part of which has been preserved, gives the following account of the scene:

"To-day, in the Church of Minerva, in the presence of the College of Cardinals and of an innumerable crowd, Molinos made his abjuration. We counted over fifty boxes in the Church filled with ladies and of the highest nobility. In other boxes were prelates, *religiosi,* seminarists, and there was not a place that was not crowded with people. Molinos was conducted to the platform facing the cardinals, and the tribunal of the Holy Office, consisting of consulting prelates, of the General of the Dominican Order, of the commissioner, of some of the qualifiers who qualified the propositions, and other agents of the Holy Office.

Molinos stood with a policeman by his side, who, from time to time, wiped his face. In his hands, which were manacled, he held a burning candle. From the pulpit near the criminal one of the fathers of St. Dominic read, in a loud voice, an abstract of the trial. It was observed that his face while this lasted, about three hours, as when he entered and left, was full of contempt and defiance, especially at the commotion of the people, who, as they heard the account of some of his graver villanies, shouted boisterously, 'To the stake! to the stake!' During all this Molinos did not even change colour, but made his feeling of contempt only the more conspicuous. He did not even bow his head when several times the names of Jesus, Mary, and the Holy Sacrament were pronounced, whence many concluded that he abjured, not from a detestation of the heresy which he heard read, but to avoid being made a spectacle of in the Campo di Fiore, where he would have been burnt alive."

Among the many notoriously unfair trials of supposed heretics, few have been so bad as this of Molinos. The charges brought against him are not founded on his writings, and his accusers were evidently aware that the charge of heresy was a flimsy one. The real charge was that he had been a man of impure life, an accusation which has never been wanting against an enemy whom the Jesuits wished to get rid of. It is said that he confessed and abjured. What words might have been wrung from him during agonies of torture in the dungeons of the Inquisition no one knows. The correspondence of his enemies, however, who wrote from Rome during the time of his examination show that he had maintained an unshaken firmness and fortitude. No more cruel or unjust charges could have been brought against any man. The real crime of Molinos in the eyes of the Jesuits was that he himself and his disciples lived pure Christian lives, and yet did not frequent the confessional, and set small store by relic-reverence, image worship, and the various superstitious rites which Romanists thought to be essential to religion. The teaching which brought upon him the attack of the Inquisition was the declaration made implicitly by all Mysticism and Quietism that there may be religion without priestcraft, and an approach to God's footstool without first kneeling at a priest's. He looked directly to God for light and grace, and that faith gave him throngs of followers who were yearning in secret to get rid of the yoke of priestly mediation which the Jesuits had by their theory and use of the confessional firmly rivetted on the neck of the nations who had not abjured Romanism at the Reformation. It is a singular evidence of the religious undercurrent of the time, of the power of the Jesuits, and of the weariness of many in the unreformed Church, that prayers were actually offered up that the Pope, who favoured Molinos, should be converted to Romanism! No one knows how far the movement might have gone, or how much purer the Christianity of the Romance nations might have become, had Molinos and Quietism not been stamped out in this ruthless fashion.

From the Church of Minerva Molinos was reconducted to his prison, which he never afterwards left. His followers were hunted out in Italy, Spain, and France, and Jesuistry triumphed. He died on December 28, 1696, in his 70th year.

> *Must we deny—do they these Molinists,*
> *At peril of their body and their soul—*
> *Recognized truths, obedient to some*
>   *truth*
> *Unrecognized yet, but perceptible?*
> *Correct the portrait by the living face,*
> *Man's God, by God's God in the mind*
>   *of man.*
> *—Browning,* Ring and the Book.
> *So when my Savior calls, I rise*
> *And calmly do my best;*
> *Leaving to Him, with silent eyes*
> *Of hope and fear, the rest.*

I step, I mount, where He has led;
Men count my haltings o'er;
I know them; yet tho' self I dread,
I love His precept more.

— *J.H. NEWMAN.*

J. HENRY SHORTHOUSE

---

1. Bigelow, *Molinos the Quietist,* p. 25.
2. Bigelow, *Molinos the Quietist,* p. 63.

PREFACE.

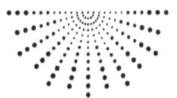

𝒶 FTER the "Life of Molinos," and before the reader forms an acquaintance with Molinos himself, my part in this little volume would seem to be small. There remains indeed only to give thanks for these

"Words of Blessing and of Peace."

For though, here and there in this little book, some things may strike us as hard sayings, yet it seems to me that this message from a foreign country and a bye-gone age is not without a singular Appropriateness at the present time, when the inquiring intellect is so much in the ascendant, and the soundings have become strange, and the old land-marks dim in the ever seething mist. For this "Method of Molinos" deals with an experience of the mind which is utterly unaffected by any of the controversies which trouble the Christian Church in these days. The Faith of which he speaks is not a Faith in a series of events or in any schemes of dogma, however important or useful such Faith may be (and I for one believe it to be very important), but the Faith of which he speaks is Faith in an eternal principle—in that awful yet gracious Presence, by whatever name we choose to call it—the Sense in every one of us of Purity and Peace, of Righteousness and Love and Power: of that Plastic Force, in short, which "inhabiteth Eternity"—with which the universe is instinct—and in which benign and intelligent energy some of us still recognise a Personal God.

When we enter, with Molinos, into the mystical state of "internal recollection and silence," we leave behind us all the perplexing questions by which religious life in the present day is disturbed. These things "cease from troubling," we find ourselves face to face with the Eternal and Ideal, and we lie still and passive if so be that He may work His gracious will on us. Is not this a blessed change from jangling and contention, from doubt and distress? and, indeed, when we come to think of it, it would seem not so strange a thing to ask, that, when we think of all the blessings which we have inherited and received, "those which we have forgotten, and those which we cherish in our memories and feel in our hearts," and of this crowning blessing by which humanity is raised to the Ideal, and the imperfect love of the least of us is made partaker, and in some sense even the pattern, of the Divine Love—when we think of the blessing which such thoughts as these have brought to the most sorrowful and careworn life—is it so strange that we should sometimes think it possible that we might all of us with all our differences and estrangements in this one thing united as children of a common Father, "evermore give thanks unto Him in His Holy Church"?

For the extracts from Molinos' book which are here given are only part of his Method, and relate only to that portion which belongs to the Mystical Theology. Molinos' Method consisted in the uniting of this spiritual experience and training with the system and worship of the Church-Catholic; and this ought not to have been found so difficult, for if we will think for a moment, we shall see that this method of the soul's training in mystical worship is in fact conceived in the purest spirit of that Sacramentalism, which has nothing to do with priest-craft, and is the basis of that Idea of the Church which all its abuses in all ages, so far from creating, have only impeded and obscured. The "prayer of silence," the "spiritual martyrdom," the "mystical peace," the "entrance into internal recollection through the most Holy Humanity of our Lord Jesus Christ," are all the offspring of the Sacramental principle, which finds an utterance in outward fact, informal and ceremonious usage and not in human intellect and speech, is nowhere so clearly seen as in the worship of the Church-Catholic in its purest form, and could nowhere, so Molinos insisted, more surely be expected than in the Communion of the constituent parts of that Holy Humanity, the Precious Body and Blood.

The brazen gates are closed behind us which shut out the fantastic throng of troublous and distracting thoughts; above and around us, in the windows and on the walls, are saints and apostles, martyrs, servants and seers who have endured to the end; sense is there, but it is sense in its ideal entirety, not the erring and wandering sense of perplexed Humanity; melodious sound is there, but inarticulate, or, if articulate, in the hallowed words of centuries, which have lost the note of finite utterance and become universal as silence itself; form is there, but form hallowed and mystical, without choice or alternative, without growth and without decay, and before the adoring individual sense, thus chastened and annihilated, is presented the God-given Humanity as God Himself restored it and offered it before the universe as a sacrifice again.

J. HENRY SHORTHOUSE

GOLDEN THOUGHTS FROM THE SPIRITUAL GUIDE WHICH DISENTANGLES THE SOUL AND BRINGS IT BY THE INWARD WAY TO THE GETTING OF PERFECT CONTEMPLATION, AND THE RICH TREASURE OF INTERNAL PEACE.

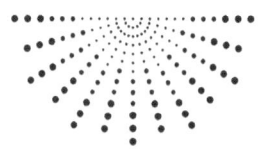

WRITTEN BY DR. MIGUEL DE MOLINOS.

The way of inward peace is in all things to be conform to the pleasure and disposition of the Divine Will. Such as would have all things succeed and come to pass according to their own fancy, are not come to know this way. And therefore lead a harsh and bitter life, always restless and out of humour, without treading in the way of peace, which consists in a total conformity to the will of God.

THE FIRST PART. OF THE DARKNESS, DRYNESS, AND TEMPTATIONS, WHEREWITH GOD PURGES SOULS, AND OF INTERNAL RECOLLECTION.

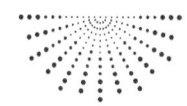

To the end God may rest in the soul, the heart is always to be kept peaceable in whatsoever disquiet, temptation, and tribulation.
We will come in unto him, and make Our abode with him.

Thou art to know that thy soul is the centre, habitation, and kingdom of God. That, therefore, to the end the sovereign King may rest on that throne of thy soul, thou oughtest to take pains to keep it clean, quiet, void and peaceable—clean from guilt and defects; quiet from fears; void of affections, desires, and thoughts; and peaceable in temptations and tribulations.

Thou oughtest always, then, to keep thine

heart in peace, that thou mayest keep pure that temple of God, and with a right and pure intention thou art to work, pray, obey, and suffer, without being in the least moved, whatever it pleases the Lord to send unto thee.

Because it is certain that for the good of the soul, and for thy spiritual profit, He will suffer the envious enemy to trouble that City of Rest, and Throne of Peace, with temptations, suggestions, and tribulations, and by the means of creatures, with painful troubles, and grievous persecutions.

Be constant, and cheer up thine heart in whatsoever disquiet these tribulations may cause to thee. Enter within it, that thou mayest overcome it, for therein is the divine fortress which defends, protects, and fights for thee. If a man hath a safe fortress he is not disquieted though his enemies pursue him, because by retreating within it these are disappointed and overcome. The strong castle that will make thee triumph over all thine enemies, visible and invisible, and over all their snares and tribulations, is within thine own soul, because in it resides the Divine Aid and Sovereign Succour.

Retreat within it and all will be quite secure, peaceable, and calm.

It ought to be thy chief and continual exercise

to pacify that throne of thy heart, that the Supreme King may rest therein.

The way to pacify it will be to enter into thyself by means of internal recollection: all thy protection is to be prayer, and a living recollection in the Divine Presence.

When thou seest thyself more sharply assaulted, retreat into that region of peace, where thou wilt find the fortress.

When thou art more faint-hearted, betake thyself to this refuge of prayer, the only armour for overcoming the enemy, and mitigating tribulation. Thou oughtest not to be at a distance from it in a storm, to the end thou mayest, like another Noah, experience tranquillity, security, and serenity, and to the end thy will may be resigned, devout, peaceful, and courageous.

Finally, be not afflicted nor discouraged to see thyself faint-hearted; He returns to quiet thee, that still He may stir thee; because this Divine Lord will be alone with thee, to rest in thy soul, and form therein a rich throne of peace; that within thine own heart, by means of internal recollection, and with His heavenly grace, thou mayest look for silence in tumult, solitude in company, light in darkness, forgetfulness in pressures, vigour in despondency, courage in fear, resistance in temptation, peace in war, and quiet in tribulation.

Though the soul perceive itself deprived of discourse or ratiocination, yet it ought to persevere in prayer, and not to be afflicted, because that is its greater felicity.
Praying always.

. . . Thou oughtest to be persuaded, that thou mayest not draw back, when thou wantest expansion and discourse in *Prayer;* that it is thy greatest happiness, because it is a clear sign that the Lord will have thee to walk by faith and silence in His divine presence, which is the most profitable and easiest path, in respect that with a simple view, or loving attention to God, the soul appears like a humble supplicant before its Lord, or as an innocent child that casts itself into the sweet and safe bosom of its dear mother.

Thus did Gerson express it: Though I have spent forty years in reading and prayer, yet I never find anything more efficacious nor compendious for attaining to the mystical theology, than that our spirit should become like a young child and beggar in the presence of God.

That kind of prayer is not only the easiest, but the most secure; because it is abstracted from the operations of the imagination that is always exposed to the tricks of the devil, and the extravagancies of melancholy and ratiocination, wherein the soul is easily distracted, and being wrapt up in speculation, reflects on itself. . . .

When God intends, after an extraordinary manner, to guide the soul into the school of the divine and loving notices of the internal law, He makes it go with darkness and dryness, that He may bring it near to Himself; because the Divine Majesty knows very well that it is not by the means of one's own ratiocination or industry that a soul draws near to Him and understands the Divine Writings, but rather by silent and humble resignation. . . .

What concerns thee most, O redeemed soul, is patience, not to desist from the prayer thou art about, though thou canst not enlarge in discourse.

Walk with firm faith, and a holy silence, dying in thyself, with all thy natural industry, trusting that God, who is the same and changes not, neither can err, intends nothing but thy good.

It is clear that he who is dying must needs feel it; but how well is time employed when the soul is dead, dumb, and resigned, in the presence of God, there without any clatter or distraction to receive the Divine influences.

The senses are not capable of Divine blessings: hence if thou wouldest be happy and wise have patience: be confident and walk on. It concerns thee far more to hold thy peace, and to let thyself be guided by the hand of God, than to enjoy all the goods of this world. And though it seem to thee that thou dost nothing at all, and art idle, being so dumb and resigned, yet it is of infinite fruit. . . .

Take care, then, that thou afflict not thyself, nor draw back, though thou canst not enlarge thyself, and discourse in prayer; suffer, hold thy peace, and appear in the presence of God; persevere constantly, and trust to His infinite bounty, who can give unto thee constant faith, true light, and divine grace.

Walk as if thou wert blindfolded, without thinking or reasoning; put thyself into His kind and paternal hands, resolving to do nothing but what His Divine Will and Pleasure is.

The soul is not to afflict itself, nor intermit prayer, because it sees itself encompassed with dryness.
My soul . . . longeth for Thee in a dry and thirsty land.

Thou shalt know that there are two sorts of prayer, the one tender, delightful, amiable, and full of sentiments; the other obscure, dry, desolate, tempted and darksome. . . .

God gives the first to gain souls, the second to purify them.

With the first He uses them like children; with the second He begins to deal with them as strong men. . . .

Know that the Lord makes use of the veil of dryness, to the end that we may not know what He is working in us, and so be humble. Because if we felt and knew what He is working in our souls, satisfaction and presumption would get in, imagining that we were doing some good thing, and reckoning ourselves very near to God, which would be our undoing. . . .

Thou oughtest not, then, to afflict thyself, nor think that thou reapest no fruit, because in coming from a communion or prayer, thou hast not the experience of many sentiments, since that is a manifest cheat. The husbandman sows in one time, and reaps in another: so God upon occasion and in His own due time will help thee to resist temptation, and when least thou thinkest, will give thee holy purposes, and more effectual desires of serving Him.

To the end thou mayest not suffer thyself to be transported by the violent suggestion of the enemy, who will enviously persuade thee, that thou dost nothing, and that thou losest time, that so thou mayest neglect prayer, I shall declare to thee some of the infinite fruits that thy soul reaps from the great dryness:—

- 1. The first is to persevere in prayer, from which fruit spring many other advantages.
- 2. Thou wilt find a loathing of the things of the world, which by little and little tends to the stifling of the bad desires of thy past life, and the producing of other new ones of serving God.
- 3. Thou wilt reflect on many failings on which formerly thou didst not reflect . . .
- 4. Thou wilt know thyself better, and be confounded also in thyself, feel in thee a high esteem of God above all created beings, a contempt of creatures, and a firm resolution not to abandon prayer, though thou knowest that it will prove to thee a most cruel martyrdom. . . .

All these and many other fruits, are like new buds that spring from the prayer which thou couldest give over, because it seems to thee to be dry. . . .

Be constant and persevere with patience, for though thou knowest it not, thy soul is profited thereby. . . .

The soul is not to be disquieted, that it sees itself encompassed with darkness, because that is an instrument of its greater felicity.
He made darkness His secret place.

There are two sorts of darkness: some unhappy and others happy.

The first are such as arise from sin, and are unhappy, because they lead the soul to an eternal precipice.

The second are those which the Lord suffers to be in the soul, to ground and settle it in virtue: and these are happy, because they enlighten it, fortify it, and cause greater light therein.

Thou oughtest not, therefore, to grieve and disturb thyself, nor be disconsolated in seeing thyself obscure and darksome, judging that God hath failed thee, and the light also that thou formerly hadst the experience of; thou oughtest rather at that time persevere constantly in prayer, it being a manifest sign that God of His infinite mercy intends to bring thee into the inward path and happy way of paradise. . . .

See now if darkness be not to be esteemed and embraced.

What thou oughtest to do amidst them, is to believe that thou art before the Lord, and in His presence; but thou oughtest to do so, with a sweet and quiet attention, nor desire to know anything, nor search after delicacies, tendernesses, or sensible devotions, nor do anything but what is the good will and pleasure of God: because otherwise thou wilt only make circles all thy life-time, and not advance one step towards perfection.

That the soul may attain to the supreme internal peace God must purge it after His own way.
He purgeth it that it may bring forth more fruit.

So soon as thou shalt firmly resolve to mortify thy external senses, that thou mayest advance towards the high mountain of union with God, His Divine Majesty will set His Hand to the purging of thy evil inclinations, inordinate desires, vain complacency, self love and pride, and other hidden vices, which thou knowest not, and which yet reign in the inner parts of thy soul, and hinder the divine union. . . .

God will do all this in thy soul by means of the cross and dryness, if thou freely givest thy consent to it by resignation, and walking through these darksome and desert ways.

All thou hast to do, is to do nothing by thine own choice alone. The subjection of thy liberty is that which thou oughtest to do, quietly resigning thyself up in everything, whereby the Lord shall think fit internally and externally to mortify thee: because that is the only means by which thy soul can become capable of the divine influences, whilst thou sufferest internal and external tribulation with humility, patience, and quiet; not the penances, disciplines, and mortifications which thou couldest impose thyself.

The husbandman sets a greater esteem upon the plants which *he* sows in the ground than upon those that spring up of themselves, because these never come to seasonable maturity.

In the same manner God esteems and is better pleased with the virtue which He sows and infuses into the soul (as being sunk into its own nothingness, calm and quiet retreated within its own centre, and without any election), than with all the other virtues which the soul pretends to acquire by its own election and endeavours.

It concerns thee only, then, to prepare thine heart like clean paper, wherein the Divine Wisdom may imprint characters to His own liking.

O how great a work will it be for thy soul to be whole hours together in prayer, dumb, resigned, and humble without acting, knowing, or desiring to understand anything.

With new efforts thou wilt exercise thyself, but in another manner than hitherto, giving thy consent to receive the secret and divine operations, to be polished and purified by the Lord, which is the only means whereby thou wilt become clean and purged from thy ignorance and dissolutions.

Know however that thou art to be plunged in a bitter sea of sorrows, and of internal and external pains, which torment will pierce into the most inward part of thy soul and body. . . .

But fear not.

All this is necessary for purging thy soul, and making it know its own misery, and sensibly perceive the annihilation of all the passions and disordinate appetites wherewith it rejoiced itself.

Finally, to the end the Lord may refine and purify thee after His own manner with those inward torments, wilt thou not cast the Jonah of sense into the sea, that thereby thou mayest procure this purity?

With all thy outward disciplines and mortifications, thou wilt never have true light, nor make one step toward perfection: thou wilt stop in the beginning, and thy soul will not attain to the amiable rest and supreme eternal peace.

The soul ought not to be disquieted . . . because it finds itself assaulted by temptation.
Blessed is the man that endureth temptation.

Our own nature is so base, proud, and ambitious, and so full of its own appetites, its own judgment and opinions, that if temptations restrained it not, it would be undone without remedy.

The Lord then, seeing our misery and perverse inclination, and thereby moved to compassion, suffers us to be assaulted by divers thoughts against the faith, horrible temptations, and by violent and painful suggestions of impatience, pride, gluttony, luxury, rage, blasphemy, cursing, despair, and an infinite number of others, to the end we may know ourselves and be humble. With these horrible temptations that Infinite Goodness humbles our pride, giving us in them the most wholesome medicine.

All our righteousness are as filthy rags, through the stains of vanity, conceitedness, and self-love. It is necessary that they may be purified with the fire of tribulation and temptation, that so they may be clean, pure, perfect, and agreeable to the eyes of God.

Therefore the Lord purifies the soul which He calls, and will have for Himself, with the rough file of temptation, with which He polishes it from the rust of pride, avarice, vanity, ambition, presumption, and self-conceit.

He pacifies and exercises it, making it to know its own misery. . . .

That thou mayest not lose internal peace it is necessary thou believe that it is the goodness of Divine Mercy when thus it humbles, afflicts, and tries thee; since by that means thy soul comes to have a deep knowledge of itself, reckoning itself the worst, most impious and abominable of all souls living, and hence with humility and lowliness it abhors itself.

O how happy would souls be if they would be quiet, and believe that all these temptations are caused by the devil, and received from the hand of God for their gain and spiritual profit.

But thou wilt say that it is not the work of the devil, when he molests thee by means of creatures, but the effects of thy neighbours' faults and malice in having wronged and injured thee.

Know that that is another cunning and hidden temptation, because though God wills not the sin of another, yet He wills His own effects in thee, and the trouble which accrues to thee from another's fault, that He may see thee improved by the benefit of patience.

Dost thou receive an injury from any man? There are two things in it, the sin of him that does it, and the punishment that thou sufferest: the sin is against the will of God, and displeases Him, though He permit it; the punishment is conform to His will, and He wills it for thy good; wherefore thou oughtest to receive it, as from His hand.

The passion and death of our Lord Jesus Christ were the effects of the wickedness and sins of Pilate, and yet it is certain that God willed the death of His Own Son for our redemption.

Consider how the Lord makes use of another's fall for the good of thy soul.

O the greatness of Divine Wisdom! Who can pry into the depth of the secret and extraordinary means, and the hidden, parts, whereby He guides the soul, which He would have purged, transformed, and made divine. . . .

Thou art to know, then, that temptation is thy great happiness: so that the more it besets thee the more thou oughtest to rejoice in peace, instead of being sad, and to thank God for the favour He does thee. . . .

The Saints, in arriving at holiness, passed through this doleful valley of temptations: and the greater Saints they were the greater temptations they grappled with. . . .

Finally, thou art to know that the greatest temptation is to be without temptation; wherefore thou oughtest to be glad when it assaults thee, and with resignation, peace, and constancy, resist it.

If thou wilt serve God, and arrive at the sublime region of internal peace, thou must pass through that rugged path of temptation. Put on that happy armour, fight in that fierce and cruel war; and in that burning furnace polish, purge, renew, and purify thyself.

Of the nature of internal recollection, and how the soul ought to behave itself therein, and of the spiritual warfare whereby the devil endeavours to disturb it at that time.
Speak, Lord, for Thy servant heareth. If we be dead with Christ we shall also live with Him.

Internal recollection is *faith and silence* in the presence of God.

Hence thou oughtest to be accustomed to recollect thyself in His presence, with an affectionate attention, as one that is given up to God, and united unto Him, with reverence, humility, and submission, beholding Him in the most inward recess of thine own soul, without form, likeness, manner, or figure. . . .

Here thou art to shut up the senses, trusting God with all the care of thy welfare, and minding nothing of the affairs of this life.

Thy faith ought to be pure, without representations or likeness; simple, without reasonings; and universal, without distinctions. . . .

Though thou canst not get rid of the anguish of thoughts, hast no light, comfort, nor spiritual sentiment: yet be not afflicted, neither leave off recollection, because they are the snares of the enemy.

Resign thyself at that time with vigour, endure with patience, and persevere in His presence: for whilst thou perseverest after that manner, thy soul will be internally improved. . . .

The fruit of true prayer consists not in enjoying the light nor in having knowledge of spiritual things, since these may be found in a speculative intellect, without true virtue and perfection. It only consists in *enduring* with patience, and persevering in faith and silence, believing that thou art in the Lord's presence, turning to Him thy heart with tranquillity and purity of mind. So whilst thou perseverest in this manner, thou wilt have the only preparation and disposition which at that time is necessary, and reap infinite fruit. . . .

As many times as thou exercisest thyself calmly to reject these vain thoughts, so many crowns will the Lord set upon thy head; and though it may seem to thee that thou dost nothing, be undeceived; for a good desire, with firmness and steadfastness in prayer, is very pleasing to the Lord. . . .

God loves not him who does most, who hears most, nor who shows greatest affection, but who suffers most, if he pray with faith and reverence, believing that he is in the Divine presence. . . .

God hath no regard to the multitude of words, but to the purity of the intent.

His greatest content and glory at that time is to see the soul in silence, desirous, humble, quiet, and resigned.

Proceed, persevere, pray, and hold thy peace, for where thou findest not a sentiment thou wilt find a door, whereby thou mayest enter into thine own nothingness, knowing thyself to be nothing, that thou canst do nothing, nay, and that thou hast not so much as a good thought. . . .

The more the soul rejoices in sensible love the less delight God has in it: on the contrary, the less the soul rejoices in this sensible love, the more God delights in it.

Know that to fix the will on God, restraining thoughts and temptations, with the greatest tranquillity possible, is the highest pitch of praying.

What the soul ought to be in internal recollection.

Wait, I say, on the Lord. It is good that a man should both hope and quietly wait for the salvation of God.

Thou oughtest to go to prayer, that thou mayest deliver thyself wholly up into the hands of God with perfect resignation, exerting an act of faith, believing that thou art in the Divine presence, afterwards settling in that holy repose with quietness, silence, tranquillity; and endeavouring for a whole day, a whole year, and thy whole life to continue that first act of contemplation by faith and love. . . .

Having once dedicated, and lovingly resigned thyself to the will of God, there is nothing else for thee to do but to continue the same, without repeating new and sensible acts, provided thou takest not back the jewel thou hast once given, by committing some notable fault against His Divine Will: though thou oughtest still to exercise thyself outwardly in the external works of thy calling and state, for in so doing thou doest the Will of

God, and walkest in continual and virtual praying.

He always prays, said Theophylact, *who does good works, nor does he neglect prayer but when he leaves off to be just.*

Thou oughtest, then, to slight all those sensible things, to the end thy soul may be established, and acquire a habit of internal recollection, which is so effectual that the resolution only of going to prayer awakens a lively presence of God, which is the preparation to the prayer that is about to be made; or, to say better, is no other than a more efficacious continuation of continual prayer, wherein the contemplative person ought to be settled...

How happy and well-applied will thy soul be, if retreating within itself it there shrinks into its own nothing, both in its centre and superior part, without minding what it does; whether it recollect or not; whether it walk well or ill; if it operate or not without heeding, thinking, or minding any sensible thing?

At that time the intellect believes with a pure act, and the will loves with perfect love, without any kind of impediment, imitating that pure and continued act of intuition and love which the saints say the blessed in heaven have, with no other difference than that they see one another there face to face, and the soul here, through the veil of an obscure faith. . . .

O that thy soul, without thoughtful advertency, even of itself, might give itself in prayer, in that holy and spiritual tranquillity.

Let it be silent and do nothing, forget itself and plunge into that obscure faith. How secure and safe would it be, though it might seem to it, that thus unactive and doing nothing, it were undone.

How the soul, putting itself in the presence of God, with perfect resignation, by the pure act of faith, walks always in virtual and acquired contemplation.

Rest in the Lord, wait patiently for Him.

Thou wilt tell me that though by a perfect resignation thou hast put thyself in the presence of God by means of pure faith, yet thou dost not improve, because thy thoughts are so distracted, that thou canst not be fixed upon God.

Be not disconsolate, for thou dost not lose time, neither desist thou from prayer; because it is not necessary that during that whole time of recollection thou shouldst actually think on God. It is enough that thou hast been attentive in the beginning: provided thou discontinue not thy purpose, nor revoke the actual attention which thou hadst. . .

The prayer still continues, though the imagination may ramble upon infinite numbers of things, provided one consent not to it, shift not place, intermit not the prayer, nor change the first intention of being with God. . . .

He prays in spirit and in truth, says Thomas Aquinas, *whoever goes to prayer with the spirit and intention of praying, though afterwards, through misery and frailty, his thoughts may wander.*

So long as thou retractest not that faith and intention of being resigned, thou walkest always in faith and resignation, and consequently in prayer, and in virtual and acquired contemplation, although thou perceive it not, remember it not, neither exertest new acts and reflections thereon. . . .

The inward soul being once resolved to believe that God is in it, and that it will not desire, nor act anything but through God, ought to rest satisfied in that faith and intention in all its works and exercises, without forming or repeating new acts of the same faith, or of such a resignation.

This true doctrine serves not only for the time of prayer, but also after it is over, by night and by day, at all hours, and in all the daily functions of thy calling, thy duty, and condition.

If thou tell me that many times thou forgettest,

during the whole day, to renew thy resignation: I answer, though it seem to thee that thou art diverted from it by attending the daily occupations of thy vocation, as studying, reading, preaching, eating, drinking, doing business, and the like, thou art mistaken, for the one destroys not the other, nor by so doing dost thou neglect to do the Will of God, nor to proceed in virtual prayer.

These occupations are not contrary to His Will, nor contrary to thy resignation: it being certain that God would have thee to eat, study, take pains, do business, and so on. So that to perform these exercises, which are conformed to His Will and Pleasure, thou departest not out of His Presence, nor from thine own resignation.

But if in prayer, or out of it, thou shouldest willingly be diverted or distracted, suffering thyself deliberately to be transported into any passion, then it will be good for thee to revert to God, and return into His Divine Presence, renewing the purest acts of faith and resignation. . . .

Strive, then, when thou comest from prayer, to the end thou mayest return to it again, not to be distracted, nor diverted, but to carry thyself with a total resignation to the Divine Will, that God may do with thee and all thine according to His heavenly pleasure, relying on Him as on a kind and loving Father.

Never recall that intention, and though thou beest taken up about the affairs of the condition wherein God hath placed thee, yet thou wilt still be in prayer, in the presence of God, and in perpetual acts of resignation. A just man leaves not off to pray unless he leaves off to be just. He always prays who always does well. The good desire is prayer, and if the desire be continued so also is the prayer. . . ..

Resignation is more perfect when it springs from the internal and infused fortitude, which grows as the internal exercise of pure faith, with silence and resignation, is continued. . . .

From all which, be persuaded, that the inward soul, accustomed to go daily at certain hours to prayer, with the faith and resignation I have mentioned to thee, walks continually in the presence of God.

A way by which we may enter into internal recollection, through the most holy Humanity of our Lord Jesus Christ.

I am the Way, the Truth, and the Life.

. . . It is certain that our Lord Christ is the guide, the door, and the way. And before the soul can be fit to enter into the presence of the Divinity, and to be united with it, it is to be washed with the Precious Blood of a Redeemer, and adorned with the rich robes of His Passion.

Our Lord Jesus Christ, with His teaching and example, is the Mirror, the Guide of the soul, the Way, and the only door by which we enter into those pastures of Life Eternal, and into the vast ocean of the divinity.

Hence it follows that the Passion and Death of our Saviour ought not to be blotted out of the remembrance: nay it is also certain that whatsoever high elevation of mind the soul may be raised to, it ought not to separate from the most holy Humanity. But then it follows not from hence neither, that the soul, accustomed to internal recollection, should always be meditating on, and considering the most holy mysteries of our Saviour. . . .

To take a secure means, then, and to avoid those two contrary extremes, of not wholly blotting out the remembrance of the Humanity, and of not having It continually before our eyes, we ought to suppose that there are two ways of attending the holy Humanity. The first is by considering the mysteries, and meditating on the actions of the life, passion, and death of our Saviour. The second, by thinking on Him, by the application of the intellect pure faith or memory.

When the soul succeeds, in perfecting and interiorising itself, by means of internal recollection, having for some time meditated on the mysteries whereof it hath been already informed: then it retains faith and love to the Word Incarnate, being ready for His sake to do whatever He inspires into it, walking according to His precepts, although they be not always before its eyes. As if it should be laid to a son, that he ought never to forsake his father, they intend not thereby to oblige him to have his father always in sight, but only to have him always in his memory, that in time and place he may be ready to do his duty. The soul, then, that is entered into internal recollection hath no need to enter by the first door of meditation on the mysteries, being always taken up in meditating upon them, because that is not to be done without great fatigue to the intellect, nor does it stand in need of such ratiocinations, since these serve only as a means to attain to believing that which it hath already got the possession of.

The most noble, spiritual, and proper way for souls that are proficient in internal recollection, to enter by the Humanity of Christ our Lord, and entertain a remembrance of Him, is the second way: eyeing that Humanity, and the Passion thereof, by a simple act of faith; working and reflecting on the same as the Tabernacle of the Divinity, the beginning and end of our salvation, Jesus Christ having been born, suffered, and died a shameful death for our sakes.

This is the way that makes internal souls profit, and this holy, pious, swift, and instantaneous remembrance of the Humanity, can be no obstacle to them in the course of internal recollection, unless if when the soul enters into prayer, it finds itself drawn back: for then it will be better to continue recollection and mental exercise. But not finding itself drawn back, the simple and swift remonstrance of the Humanity of the Divine Word, gives no impediment to the highest and most elevated, the most abstracted and transformed soul. . . .

Let the soul, then, when it enters into recollection, place itself at the gate of Divine Mercy, which is the amiable and sweet remembrance of the Cross and Passion of the Word that was made Man and died for Love. Let it stand there with humility, resigned to the Will of God, in whatsoever it pleases the Divine Majesty to do with it: and if, from that holy and sweet remembrance, it soon falls into forgetfulness, there is no necessity of making a new repetition. Only continue silent and quiet in the presence of the Lord.

Of internal and mystical silence.

My little children, let us not love in word neither in tongue, but in deed and in truth.

There are three kinds of silence; the first is of words, the second of desires, and the third of thoughts. The first is perfect, the second more perfect, and the third is most perfect.

In the first, that is, of words, virtue is acquired: in the second, to wit of desires, quietness is attained to: in the third, of thoughts, internal recollection is gained.

By not speaking, nor desiring, and not thinking, one arrives at the true and perfect mystical silence, wherein God speaks with the soul, communicates Himself to it, and in the abyss of its own depth, teaches it the most perfect and exalted wisdom.

He calls and guides it to this inward solitude and mystical silence, when He says that He will speak to it alone, in the most secret and hidden part of the heart.

Thou art to keep thyself in this mystical silence if thou wouldest hear the sweet and divine voice. It is not enough, for gaining this treasure to forsake the world, nor to renounce thine own desires, and all things created, if thou wean not thyself from all desires and thoughts.

Rest in this mystical silence and open the door that so God may communicate Himself unto thee, unite with thee, and then form thee unto Himself.

The perfection of the soul consists not in speaking, nor in thinking much on God, but in loving Him sufficiently.

This love is attained by means of perfect resignation and internal silence.

The love of God hath but few words. St. John the evangelist confirms and inculcates it thus: *My little children, let us not love in word neither in tongue, but in deed and in truth.*

. . . That a rational creature may understand the secret desire and intention of thy heart, there is a necessity that thou shouldest express it to him in words. But God who searches the heart, standest not in need that thou shouldest make profession, and assure Him of it; nor does He rest satisfied, as the evangelist says, with love in word or in tongue, but with that which is true and in deed.

What avails it to tell Him with great zeal and fervour that thou tenderly and perfectly lovest Him above all things, if at one bitter word, or slight injury thou dost not resign thyself, nor art mortified for the love of Him? A manifest proof that thy love was a love of tongue and not in deed.

Strive to be resigned in all things with silence, and in so doing, without *saying* that thou lovest Him, thou wilt attain to the most perfect, quiet, and effectual and true love.

St. Peter most affectionately told the Lord, that for His sake he was ready willingly to lay down his life: but at the word of a young damsel he denied Him, and there was an end of his zeal.

Mary Magdalen said not a word, and yet the Lord Himself, taken with her perfect love, became her panegyrist, saying that she had loved much.

It is internally, then, that with dumb silence, the most perfect virtues of Faith, Hope, and Charity are practised, without any necessity of telling God that thou lovest Him, hopest and believest in Him: because the Lord knows better than thou dost what the internal motions of thy heart are. . . .

THE SECOND PART. OF SPIRITUAL MARTYRDOMS WHEREBY GOD PURGES SOULS: OF CONTEMPLATION INFUSED AND PASSIVE: OF PERFECT RESIGNATION, INWARD HUMILITY, DIVINE WISDOM, TRUE CONCILIATION, AND INTERNAL PEACE.

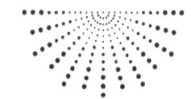

The difference between the outward and the inward man.

Apart from Me ye can do nothing.

There are two sorts of spiritual persons, internal and external: these seek God without by discourse, by imagination and consideration; they endeavour mainly to get virtues, by many abstinences, maceration of body and mortification of the senses; they give themselves to rigorous penance; they put on sack-cloth, chastise the flesh by discipline, endeavour silence, bear the Presence of God, forming Him present to themselves in their idea or imagination of Him, sometimes as a Pastor, sometimes as a Physician, and sometimes as a Father and Lord; they delight to be continually seeking of God, very often making fervent acts of love; and all this is art and meditation: by this way they desire to be great, and by the power of voluntary and exterior mortification they go in quest of sensible affections and warm sentiments, thinking that God resides only in them when they have them.

This is the external way, and the way of beginners: and though it be good, yet there is no arriving at perfection by it; nay, there is not so much as one step towards it, as experience shows in many, that, after fifty years of this external exercise, are void of God and full of themselves, having nothing of a spiritual man, but just the name of such.

There are others truly spiritual, who have passed by the beginnings of the interior way which leads to union with God, and to which the Lord called them by His Infinite Mercy, from that outward way in which before they exerted themselves.

These men retired in the inward part of their souls with true resignation into the hands of God, with a total putting off and forgetting even of themselves, do always go with a raised spirit to the presence of the Lord by means of pure faith, without image, form, or figure, but with great assurance founded in tranquillity and rest internal. In whose infused meeting and entertainment the spirit draws with so much force that it makes the soul, the heart, the body, and all the powers of it contract inwardly.

These souls have already procured themselves a greater light, and a true knowledge of Christ our Lord, both of His Divinity and His Humanity. They exercise this infused knowledge with a quiet silence in the inward entertainments and the superior part of their souls. With a spirit free from images and external recollections, with a love that is pure and stripped of all creatures, they are raised also from outward actions to the love of Humanity and Divinity; so much as they enjoy, they forget; and in all of it they find that they love their God with all their heart and spirit.

These blessed and sublimated souls take no pleasure in anything of the world, but in contempt and in being alone, and in being forsaken and forgotten by everybody. . . .

There is no news that afflicts them; no success

that makes them glad; tribulation never disturbs them; nor interior continual and Divine communication make them vain and conceited. They remain always full of holy and filial fear, in a wonderful peace, constancy, and serenity.

In the external way they take care to do continual acts of all the virtues one after another, to get to the attainment of them; they pretend to purge imperfections with industries; they take care to root up interests one after another, with a different and contrary exercise. But though they endeavour never so much, they arrive at nothing, because we cannot do anything which is not imperfection and misery.

But in the inward way, and loving entertainment in the Presence Divine, as the Lord is He that works, virtue is established, interests are rooted up, imperfections are destroyed, and passions removed; which makes the soul free unexpectedly, without so much as thinking of the good which God in His infinite mercy prepared for them.

It must be known that these souls, though thus perfect, as they have the true light of God, yet by it know profoundly their own miseries, weaknesses, and imperfections, and what they yet need to arrive at the perfection towards which they are walking; they are afflicted, and abhor themselves;

they exercise themselves in a loving fear of God, and contempt of themselves, and with a true hope in God, they distrust confidence in themselves.

The more they are humble with true contempt and knowledge of themselves, the more they please God and arrive at a singular respect and veneration in His Presence.

Of all the good works that they do, and of all that they continually suffer, as well within as without, they make no manner of account before that Divine Presence.

Their continual exercise is, to enter into themselves, in God, in the quiet and silence, because there is His centre, habitation, and delight.

They make a greater account of this interior retirement than of speaking of God; they retire into that interior and secret centre of the soul, to know God, and receive His Divine influence with fear and loving reverence; if they go out, they go out only to know and despise themselves.

But know, that few are the souls which arrive at this happy state; because few there are that are willing to embrace contempt, and suffer themselves to be refined and purified; upon which account, although there are many that enter into this interior way, yet it is a rare thing for a soul to go on, and not stop short at the entrance. . . .

The means of obtaining peace internal, is not the delight of sense; not spiritual consolation, but the denying of self-love.

He that will come after Me, let him deny himself.

It is the saying of St. Bernard, that to serve God is nothing else but to do good and suffer evil. He that would go to perfection by the means of sweetness and consolation, is mistaken; you must desire no other consolation from God than to end your life for His sake, in the state of true obedience and subjection.

Christ our Lord's way was not that of sweetness and softness, nor did He invite us to any such, either by His words or example, when He said:—*He that will come after Me, let him deny himself, and let him take up his cross and follow Me* (St. Matt. xxiv. 26).

The soul that would be united to Christ, must be conformable to Him, and follow Him in the way of suffering. . . .

Open thine eyes, and consider that . . . Christ our Lord has not invited us to follow the sweetness of our own will, but the denying of ourselves, saying: *Let him deny himself.* As if He should say, He that will follow Me, and come into perfection, let him part with his own will wholly, and leaving all things, let him entirely submit to the yoke of obedience and subjection, by means of self-denial, which is the truest cross. . . .

O what a great happiness is it for a soul to be subdued and subject! what great riches is it to be poor! what a mighty honour to be despised! what a height is it to be beaten down! what a comfort is it to be afflicted! what a credit of knowledge is it to be reputed ignorant! and finally, what a happiness of happinesses is it to be crucified with Christ! This is that lot which the Apostle gloried in, *God forbid that I should glory save in the Cross of our Lord Jesus Christ* (Gal. vi. 14).

Let others boast in their riches, dignities, delights, and honours: but to us there is no higher honour than to be denied, despised, and crucified with Christ. . . .

To deny one's self in all things, to be subject to another's judgment, to mortify continually all inward passions, to annihilate one's self in all respects, to follow always that which is contrary to one's own will, appetite, and judgment, are things that few can do; many are those that teach them, but few are they that practice them.

May it please God, that the souls which have had light, and have been called to an inward peace, and by not being constant in dryness, and tribulation and temptation, have started back, may not be cast into outward darkness, with him that had not on him a wedding-garment . . . giving himself up to self love.

This monster must be vanquished, this seven-headed beast of self love must be beheaded in order to get up to the top of the high mountain of peace.

This monster puts his head everywhere: . . . sometimes it cleaves to spiritual pleasures, staying even in the gifts of God, and in His graces freely bestowed: sometimes it desires exceedingly the preservation of health, and with disguise to be used well, its own profit and conveniences: sometimes it would seem well with very curious subtilities: and lastly, it cleaves with a notable propensity, to its own proper judgment and opinion in all things, the roots of which are closely fixed in its own will.

All these are effects of self love, and if they be not denied, it is impossible that a man should ever get up to the height of perfect contemplation, to the highest happiness of the loving union and lofty throne of peace internal.

Of two spiritual martyrdoms, wherewith God cleanseth the soul that He unites with Himself.

They cried unto the Lord in their trouble, and He delivered them out of their distresses.

Now you shall know that God uses two ways for cleansing the souls which He would perfect and enlighten to unite them closely to Himself.

The first is with the bitter waters of affliction, anguish, distress, and inward torments.

The second is with the burning fire of an inflamed love, a love impatient and hungry.

Sometimes He makes use of both in those souls which He would fill with perfection. Sometimes He puts them into the strong steeping of tribulation, and inward and outward bitterness, scorching them with the fire of rigorous temptation: sometimes He puts them into the crucible of anxious and distrustful love, making them fast there with a mighty force. . . .

O that thou wouldest understand the great good of tribulation!

This is what cleanses the soul, and produces patience; this in prayer inflames and enlarges it, and puts it upon the exercise of this most sublime act of charity.

This rejoices the soul, brings it near to God, calls it to, and gives it entrance into heaven.

This tries the true servants of God, and renders them sweet, valiant, and constant; it makes God hear them with speed....

This is the means which the Lord makes use of to humble the soul, to annihilate it, to spend it, to mortify it, to deny it, to perfect it, and fill it with His Divine gifts.

By this means of temptation and tribulation He comes to crown it, and transform it.

Know that this Lord hath his repose nowhere but in quiet souls, and in those in which the fire of tribulation and temptation hath burnt up the dregs of passions and the bitter water of afflictions hath washed off the filthy spots of inordinate appetites; in a word, this Lord reposes not Himself anywhere but where quietness reigns and self love is banished.

... This disposition of preparing the soul in its bottom for divine entrance must of necessity be made by the Divine wisdom. If a seraph is not sufficient to purify the soul, how shall a soul that is frail, miserable, and without experience, ever be able to purify itself.

Therefore the Lord Himself will dispose thee and prepare thee passively by a way thou understandest not, with the fire of tribulation and inward torment, without any other disposition on thy side than a consent to the internal and external cross.

Thou wilt find within thyself a passive dryness, darkness, anguish, contradiction, continual resistance, inward desertion, horrible desolation, continual and strong suggestion, and vehement temptation of the enemy; finally, thou wilt see thyself so afflicted that thou wilt not be able to lift up thy heart, being full of sorrow and heaviness, nor do the least act of faith, hope, or charity. . . .

But though thou shalt see thyself so oppressed, seeming to thyself to be proud, impatient, and wrathful, yet these temptations shall lose their force and power upon thee; they have no place in thy soul, by secret virtue, the sovereign gift of inward strength, which rules in the inmost part of it, conquering the most affrightening punishment and pain, and the strongest temptation.

Keep constant, O blessed soul, keep constant! for it will not be as thou imaginest, nor art thou at any time nearer to God than in such cases of desertion; for although the sun is hid in the clouds, yet it changes not its place, nor a jot the more loses its brightness.

The Lord permits this painful desertion in thy soul, to purge and polish thee, to cleanse and disrobe thee of thyself; and thou mayest in this manner be all His, and give thyself wholly to Him, as His infinite bounty is entirely given to thee, that thou mayest be His delight; for although thou dost groan and lament and weep, yet He is joyful and glad in the most secret and hidden places of thy soul.

How important it is to suffer blindfold this spiritual martyrdom.
Whom the Lord loveth He chasteneth.

... The happy souls which are guided by God, by the secret way of the interior walk and of purgative contemplation, must suffer above all strong and horrible temptations and torments, more bitter than those wherewith the martyrs were crowned in the Primitive Church.

The martyrs, besides the shortness of their torment, which hardly endured days, were comforted with a clear light and special help, in hope of the near and sure reward.

But the desolate soul that must die in itself, and put off and make clean its heart, seeing itself abandoned by God, surrounded by temptations, darkness, anguish, affliction, sorrow, and rigid doubts, doth taste of death every moment in its painful temptations and tremendous desolation, without feeling the least comfort, with an affliction so great that the pain of it seems nothing else than a death prolonged, and a continual martyrdom. . . .

Thy sorrow will seem to thee insuperable, and thine afflictions past the power of comfort, and that heaven rains no more upon thee.

Thou wilt see thyself begirt with grief, and besieged with sorrows internal, from the darkness of thy power, from the weakness of discourses.

Strong temptations will afflict thee, painful distrusts, and troublesome scruples; nay, light and judgment will forsake thee.

But if thou, O blessed soul, shouldest know how much thou art beloved and defended by that Divine Lord, in the midst of thy long torments, thou wouldest find them so sweet that it would be necessary that God should work a miracle to let thee live.

Be constant, O happy soul, be constant and of good courage: for however intolerable thou art to thyself, yet thou wilt be protected, enriched, and beloved by that greatest Good, as if He had nothing else to do than to lead thee to perfection by the highest steps of love; and if thou dost not turn away, but perseverest constantly, without leaving off thy undertaking, know that thou offerest to God the most acceptable sacrifice; so that if this Lord were capable of pain He would find no ease till He has completed this loving union with thy soul.

Afflict not thyself too much, and with inquietude, because these sharp martyrdoms may continue.

Persevere in humility, and go not out of thyself to seek aid, for all thy good consists in being silent, suffering, and holding patience with rest and resignation.

There wilt thou find the Divine strength to overcome so hard a warfare.

He is within thee that fighteth for thee, and He is strength itself. . . .

The fire of Divine Love which burns the soul.
Love is strong as death.

The other more profitable martyrdom in souls already advanced in perfection and deep contemplation is a fire of Divine Love, which burns the soul and makes it painful with the same love.

Sometimes the absence of its beloved afflicts it, sometimes the sweet, ardent, and welcome weight of the loving and Divine Presence torments it.

This sweet martyrdom always makes it sigh. Sometimes if it enjoys and has its Beloved, for the pleasure of having Him; so that it cannot contain itself: other times, if He does not manifest Himself, through the ardent anxiety of seeking, finding, and enjoying Him.

All this is the panting, suffering, and dying for love. . . .

Just so much as light and love increases, just so much increases the grief in seeking that Good absent, which it loves so well.

To feel It near itself is enjoyment, and never to have done knowing and possessing It consumes its life.

It has food and drink near its mouth whilst it wants either, and cannot be satisfied.

It sees itself swallowed up and drowned in a sea of love, whilst the Powerful Hand that is able to save it is near it, and yet doth not do it; nor doth it know when He will come whom it so much does desire.

Sometimes it hears the inward Voice of its Beloved which courts and calls it; and a soft, delicate whisper, which goes forth from the secret of the soul, where it abides, which pierces it strongly, even like to melt and dissolve it, in seeing how near it hath Him within itself, and yet how far off from it, whilst it cannot come to possess Him.

This intoxicates it, debases it, scares it, and fills it with unsatisfiableness; and therefore love is said to be strong as death, whilst it kills just as that doth.

Inward mortification and perfect resignation are necessary for obtaining internal peace.
I count all things but loss for the excellency of the knowledge of Christ Jesus my Lord.

The most subtle arrow that is shot at us from nature is to induce us to that which is unlawful, with a pretence that it may be necessary and useful.

O how many souls have suffered themselves to be led away, and have lost the Spirit by this gilded cheat. . . .

Resign and deny thyself wholly, for though true self-denial is harsh at the beginning, it is easy in the middle, and becomes most sweet in the end. . . .

In the time of strong temptation, desertion, and desolation, it is necessary for thee to get close into thy centre, that thou mayest only look at and contemplate God, who keeps His Throne and His Abode in the bottom of thy soul. . . .

True love is known, with its effects, when the

soul is profoundly humbled and desires to be truly mortified and despised....

The bottom of our souls, you will know, is the place of our happiness. There the Lord shows us wonders. There we engulf and lose ourselves in the immense ocean of His infinite goodness, in which we are kept fixed and immovable....

The spiritual man that lives by God and in Him is inwardly contented in the midst of his adversities, because the cross and affliction are his life and delight....

There must be tribulation to make a man's life acceptable unto God: without it, it is like the body without the soul, the soul without grace, the earth without the sun....

You must know that the Lord will not manifest Himself in thy soul till it be denied in itself, and dead in its senses and powers. Nor will it ever come to this state till, being perfectly resigned, it resolves to be with God alone, making an equal account of gifts and contempts, light and darkness, peace and war.

In sum, that the soul may arrive at perfect quietness, and supreme and internal peace, it ought first to die in itself, and live only in God and for Him; and the more dead it shall be in itself, the more shall it know God....

How happy wilt thou be if thou hast no other thought but to die in thyself.

Thou wilt then become not only victorious over thine enemies, but over thyself; in which victory thou wilt certainly find pure love, perfect peace, and divine wisdom. . . .

The true lesson of the spiritual man, and that which thou oughtest to learn, is to leave all things in their place, and not meddle with any but what thy office may bind thee to; because the soul which leaves everything to find God doth then begin to have all in the Eternity it seeks. . . .

Enjoyment and internal peace are the fruits of the Spirit Divine; and no man gets them into his possession if in the closet of his soul he is not a resigned man. . . .

Mortify thyself in not judging ill of anybody at any time, because the suspicion of thy neighbours disturbs the purity of heart, discomposes it, brings the soul out, and takes away its repose. . . .

Finally, be of hope, suffer, be silent and patient; let nothing affright thee: all of it will have a time to end: God only is He that is unchangeable: patience brings a man everything.

He that hath God hath all things; and he that hath Him not hath nothing.

For the obtaining of eternal peace it is necessary for the soul to know its misery.
When I am weak then am I strong.

If the soul should not fall into some faults it would never come to understand its own misery, though it hears men speak and reads spiritual books; nor can it ever obtain precious peace if it do not know first its own miserable weakness.

God will suffer in thee sometimes one fault sometimes another, that by this knowledge of thyself, seeing thee so often fallen, thou mayest believe that thou art a mere nothing; in which knowledge and belief true peace and perfect humility is founded. . . .

Thou wouldest be patient, but with another's patience; and if the impatience still continues, thou layest the blame with much pain upon thy companion without considering that thou art intolerable to thyself, and when the rancour is over thou cunningly dost return to make thyself virtuous, relating spiritual sayings with artifice of wit, without mending thy past faults.

Although thou willingly dost condemn thyself, reproving thy faults before others, yet this thou dost, more to justify thyself with him that sees thy faults, that thou mayest return again afresh to the former esteem of thyself, than through any effect of perfect humility. . . .

These are all industrious engines of self-love, and the secret pride of thy soul.

Know, therefore, that self-love reigns in thee, and that it is thy greatest hindrance from the purchasing this precious peace.

What is the false humility, and what is the true; with the effects of them?

I dwell with him also that is of a contrite and humble spirit.

Thou must know that there are two sorts of humility: one false and counterfeit, the other true.

The false one is theirs, who, like water which must mount upwards, receive an external fall and artificial submission, to rise up again immediately.

These avoid esteem and honour, that so they may be taken to be humble.

They say of themselves that they are very evil, that they may be thought good.

This is dissembled humility, and feigned, and nothing but secret pride.

Theirs is the true humility which have gotten a

perfect habit of it; they never think of it, but judge humbly of themselves.

They do things with courage and patience: they live and die in God: they do not mind themselves nor the creatures: they are constant and quiet in all things: they suffer molestation with joy, desiring more of it, that they may imitate their dear despised Jesus. . . There is no honour that they look after, nor injury to disturb them: no trouble to vex them: no prosperity to make them proud, because they are always immovable in their nothingness and in themselves with absolute peace.

The true humility doth not consist in external acts, in taking the lowest place, in going in poor clothes, in speaking submissively, in shutting the eyes, in affectionate sighings, nor in condemning thy ways, calling thyself miserable to give others to understand that thou art humble.

It consists only in the contempt of thyself, and the desire to be despised, with a low and profound knowledge, without concerning thyself whether thou art esteemed humble or no.

The torment of light, wherewith the Lord with His graces enlightens the soul, doth two things: it discovers the greatness of God, and at the same time the soul knows its own misery, in so much that no tongue is able to express the depth in which it is overwhelmed, being desirous that every one should know its humility; and it is so far from vain-glory and complacency, as it sees that grace of God to be mere goodness of Him, and nothing but His mercy which is pleased to take pity on it....

The degrees of humility are the qualities of a body in the grave: that is, to be in the lowest place, buried like one's dead, to be corrupted to itself, to be dust, and be nothing in one's own account.

Finally, if thou wouldest be blessed, learn to despise thyself and to be despised by others.

Maxims to know a simple, humble, and true heart.

Lord, my heart is not haughty, nor mine eyes lofty: neither do I exercise myself in great matters, nor in things too high for me.

Encourage thyself to be humble, embracing tribulations as instruments of thy good; rejoice in contempt, and desire that God may be thy holy refuge, comfort, and protection.

None, let him be never so great in this world, can be greater than he that is in the eye and favour of God; and therefore the truly humble man despises whatever there is in the world, even to himself, and puts his trust and repose in God. . . .

The truly humble man finds God in all things, so that whatever contempt, injury, or affront comes to him by means of creatures, he receives it with great peace and quiet internal, as sent from the Divine hand, and greatly loves the instrument with which the Lord tries him. . . .

The humble heart is not disquieted by imperfections: though these do grieve it to the soul, because they are against its loving God. Nor is he concerned that he cannot do great things: for he always stands in his own nothingness and misery. Nay, he wonders at himself that he can do anything of virtue, and presently thanks the Lord for it, with a true knowledge that it is the God that doth all, and remains dissatisfied with what he does himself. . . .

The happy soul, which is gotten to this holy hatred of itself, lives overwhelmed, drowned and swallowed up in the depth of its own nothingness, out of which the Lord raises him by communicating Divine wisdom to him, and filling him with light, peace, tranquillity, and love.

Inward solitude is that which chiefly brings a man to the purchase of internal peace.

I will bring her into the wilderness, and speak comfortably unto her.

. . . Internal solitude consists in the forgetting of the creatures, in disengaging one's self from them, in a perfect nakedness of all the affections, desires, thoughts, and one's own will. This is the true solitude, where the soul reposes with a sweet and inward serenity in the arms of its chiefest Good.

O what infinite room is there in a soul that is arrived at this divine solitude. . . . There the Lord converses, and communicates Himself inwardly with the soul; there He fills it with Himself because it is empty, clothes it with light and with His love, because it is naked, lifts it up, because it is low, and unites it with Himself, and transforms it, because it is alone. . . .

If thou wouldest enter into this heaven on earth, forget every care and every thought, get out of thyself, that the love of God may dwell in thy soul.

Live as much as ever thou canst abstracted from the creatures, dedicate thyself wholly to thy Creator, and offer thyself in sacrifice with peace and quietness of spirit.

Know that the more the soul dissolves itself,

the more way it makes into this interior solitude, and becomes clothed with God, and the more lonesome and empty of itself the soul gets to be, the more the Divine Spirit fills it. . . .

Go on without stop towards this blessedness of internal solitude; see how God calls thee to enter into thy inward centre, where He will renew thee, change thee, fill thee, clothe thee, and show thee a new heavenly kingdom, full of joy, peace, content, and serenity.

Infused and passive contemplation, and its wonderful effects.
Surely I have behaved and quieted myself.

When once the soul efficaciously embraces internal and external mortification, and is willing to die heartily to its passions and its own ways, then God uses to take it alone by itself, and raise it more than it knows to a complete repose, where He sweetly and inwardly infuses into it His light, His love, and His strength, inkindling and inflaming it with a true disposition to all manner of virtue. . . .

There the soul raised and lifted up to this passive state becomes united to its Greatest Good, without costing it any trouble or pains for this union.

There in that supreme region and sacred temple of the soul that Greatest Good takes its complacency, manifests itself, and creates a relish from the creature in a way above sense and all human understanding.

There also only the pure Spirit, who is God, rules it, and gets the mastership of it, communicating to it its illustrations and those sentiments which are necessary for the most pure and perfect union....

A simple, pure, infused, and perfect contemplation, therefore, is a known and inward manifestation which God gives of Himself, of His goodness, of His peace, of His sweetness, whose object is God, pure, unspeakable, abstracted from all particular thoughts within an inward silence.

But it is God that delights us, God that draws us, God that sweetly raises us in a spiritual and most pure manner: an admirable gift which the Divine Majesty bestows to whom He will, as He will, when He will, and for what time He will, though the state of this life be rather a state of the cross, of patience, of humility, and of suffering, than of enjoying....

God doth not always communicate Himself

with equal abundance in this sweetest and infused contemplation.

Sometimes He grants this grace more than He doth at other times; and sometimes He expects not that the soul should be so dead and denied, because this gift being His mere grace He gives it when He pleases, and as He pleases, so that no general rule can be made of it, nor any rate set to His Divine Greatness; nay, by means of this very contemplation He comes to deny it, to annihilate and die.

Sometimes the Lord gives greater light to the understanding, sometimes greater love to the will.

There is no need here for the soul to take any pains or trouble; it must receive what God gives it, and rest united, as He will have it; because His Majesty is Lord, and in the very time that He lays it asleep He possesses and fills it, and works in it powerfully and sweetly, without any industry or knowledge of its own, insomuch that before even it is aware of this so great mercy it is gained, convinced, and changed already. . . .

At no time must thou look at the effects which are wrought in thy soul, but especially herein, because it would be a hindrance to the Divine operations, which enrich it so to do: all that thou hast to do is to pant after indifference, resignation, forgetfulness; and without thy being sensible of it, the Greatest Good will leave in thy soul a fit disposition for the practice of virtue, a true love of thy cross, of thine own contempt, of thy annihilation, and greater and stronger desires still of thy greater perfection, and the most pure and affective union.

Of the two means whereby the soul ascends up to infused contemplation, with the implication of what and how many the steps of it are.

My soul waiteth for the Lord more than they that watch for the morning.

The means whereby the soul ascends to the felicity of contemplation and affective love are two: the pleasure and the desire of it.

God uses at first to fill the soul with sensible pleasures, because it is so frail and miserable that without this preventive consolation it cannot take wing towards the fruition of heavenly things.

In this first step it is disposed by contrition and is exercised in repentance, meditating upon the Redeemer's passion, working out diligently all worldly desires and vicious courses of life: because the kingdom of heaven suffers violence, and the faintheart, the delicate, never conquer it, but those that use violence and force with themselves.

The second is the desire.

The more the things in heaven are delighted in, the more they are desired; and from thence there do ensue spiritual pleasures, desires of enjoying heavenly and divine blessings, and contempt of worldly ones.

From these desires arises the inclination of following Christ our Lord; and the steps of His imitation, by which a man must go up, are *Charity, Humility, Meekness, Patience, Poverty, Self-Contempt,* the *Cross, Prayer,* and *Mortification.*

The steps of infused contemplation are three—

- The *first* is *Satiety:* when the soul is filled with God then it is quiet, and satisfied with Divine Love.
- The *second* is *Intoxication,* an elevation of soul arising from Divine Love, and Satiety in it.
- The *third* is *Security.* This step casteth out fear. The soul is so drenched with love divine, and so resigned in such a manner to the divine good pleasure, that it would willingly go to hell if it did know it so to be the Will of the Most High. . .

There are six other steps of contemplation,

which are, *Fire, Union, Elevation, Illumination, Pleasure,* and *Repose.*

With the first the soul is enkindled; and being enkindled, is anointed; being anointed, is raised; being raised, contemplates; contemplating, it receives pleasure; and receiving pleasure, it finds repose.

By these steps the soul rises higher, being abstracted and experienced in the spiritual and internal way. . . .

Signs to know the inner man, and the mind that is purged.

Neither do I exercise myself in great matters nor in things too high for me.

The signs to know the inner man by are four:—

- The *first,* if the understanding produce no other thoughts than those which stir up the light of faith; and the will is so habituated that it begets no other acts of love, than of God and in order to Him.
- The *second,* if when he ceases from an external work, in which he was employed, the understanding and the

will are presently and easily turned to God.
- The *third,* if in entering upon prayer he forgets all outward things, as if he had not seen nor used them.
- The *fourth,* if he carries himself orderly towards outward things, as if he were entering into the world again, fearing to embroil himself in business. . . .

By three signs is a mind that is purged to be known:—

- The *first* is *Diligence,* which is a strength of the mind that banishes all neglect and sloth, that it may be disposed with earnestness and confidence to the pursuit of virtue.
- The *second* is *Severity,* which likewise is a strength of mind against concupiscence, accompanied with an ardent love of roughness, vileness, and holy poverty.
- The *third* is *Benignity* and *sweetness of mind,* which drives away all rancour, envy, aversion, and hatred against one's neighbour.

Till the mind be purged, the affection purified, the memory naked, the understanding brightened, the will denied and set afire, the soul can never arrive at intimate and affective union with God. . . .

Of Divine Wisdom.
If any one of you thinketh that he is wise among you . . . let him become a fool, that he may become wise.

. . . The sermons of men of learning, who lack the Spirit, though they are made up of divers narratives, elegant descriptions, acute discourses, and exquisite proofs, yet are by no means the Word of God, but the words of men. . . .

Those that preach with zeal and sincerity preach for God; those that preach without them, preach for themselves.

Those that preach the Word of God with the Spirit make it take impression in the heart; but those that preach it without the Spirit carry it no further than to the ear.

Perfection doth not consist in teaching but in doing; because he is neither the greatest saint, nor the wisest man, that knows the truth most, but he that practises it.

It is a constant maxim that divine wisdom

begets humility; and that which is acquired by the learned begets pride.

Holiness doth not consist in forming deep and subtle conceits of the knowledge and attributes of God, but in the love of God, and in self-denial. . . .

There are two ways that lead to the knowledge of God: the one remote, the other near; the first is called *speculation,* the second *contemplation.* . . .

Many seek God and find Him not, because they are more moved by curiosity than by sincere, pure, and upright intention. They rather desire spiritual comfort than God Himself; and as they seek Him not with truth, they neither find God nor spiritual pleasures.

The spirit of Divine Wisdom fills men with sweetness, governs them with courage, and enlightens those with excellence who are subject to its direction.

Where the divine spirit dwells there is always simplicity and holy liberty. . . .

Of true and perfect annihilation.
Whom have I in heaven but Thee, and there is none on earth that I desire besides Thee.

Thou must know that all this fabric of *annihilation* hath its foundation but in two principles.

The first is to keep oneself and all worldly things in a low esteem and value: from whence the putting in practice of this self-divesting, and of self-renunciation, and forsaking of all created things, must have its rise, and that with affection and in deed.

The second principle is a great esteem of God, to love, adore, and follow Him, without the least interest of one's own, let it be never so holy.

From these two principles arise a full conformity to the Divine Will.

This powerful and practical conformity to the Divine Will in all things leads the soul to annihilation and transformation with God. . . .

This annihilation, to make it perfect in the soul, must be in a man's own judgment, in his will, in his works, inclinations, desires, thoughts, and in himself: so that the soul must find itself dead to its will, desire, endeavour, understanding, and thought; willing as if it did not will; desiring as if it did not desire; understanding as if it did not understand; thinking as if it did not think; without inclining to anything; embracing equally contempt and honours, benefits and corrections.

O what a happy soul is that which is thus dead and annihilated! It lives no longer in itself, because God lives in it.

And now it may most truly be said of it, that it

is a renewed Phoenix, because it is changed, spiritualised, transformed, and made divine.

This nothing is the ready way to obtain purity of soul, perfect contemplation, and the rich treasure of peace internal.
Ye are dead, and your life is hid with Christ in God.

. . . We seek ourselves every time we get out of our *nothing:* and therefore we never get quiet and perfect contemplation.

Creep in as far as ever thou canst into the truth of thy *nothing,* and then nothing will disquiet thee. . . .

By the way of *nothing* thou must come to lose thyself in God (which is the last degree of perfection), and happy wilt thou be if thou canst so use thyself: then thou wilt get thyself gain, and find thyself most certainly. . . .

What a treasure thou wilt find if thou shalt once fix thy habitation in nothing! And if thou settest but into the centre of nothing, thou wilt never concern thyself with anything without . . . nothing will vex thee or break thy peace. . . With the helmet of *nothing* thou wilt be too hard for strong temptations and the terrible suggestions of the envious enemy. . . .

By this gate thou must enter into the happy land of the living, where thou wilt find the greatest good, the breadth of charity, the beauty of righteousness, the strait line of equity and justice.

Lastly, do not look at *nothing*, desire *nothing*, will *nothing*, endeavour *nothing;* and then *in everything* thy soul will live reposed with quiet and enjoyment.

This is the way to get purity of soul, perfect contemplation, and peace internal.

Walk therefore in this safe path, and endeavour to overwhelm thyself in this *nothing*, endeavour to use thyself, to sink deep into it, if thou hast a mind to be annihilated, united, and transformed.

Of the high felicity of internal peace, and the wonderful effects of it.

Unto Thee I lift up mine eyes, O Thou that dwellest in the heavens.

The soul being once annihilated and renewed with perfect nakedness finds in its superior part a profound peace, and a sweet rest, which brings it to such a union of love that it is joyful all over.

And such a soul as this is already arrived to

such a happiness that it neither wills nor desires anything but what its Beloved wills.

It conforms itself to this will in all emergencies, as well in comfort as in anguish, and rejoices also in everything to do the Divine good pleasure. . . .

O happy soul that enjoys here on earth so great a felicity! Thou must know that these kind of souls (though few they are) be the strong pillars which support the church, and such as abate the Divine indignation.

This [internal peace] is the rich and hidden treasure; this is the blessed, true, and happy life, and the blessedness here below.

O thou lovely greatness that passest the knowledge of the sons of men.

O excellent supernatural life, how admirable and unspeakable art thou: for thou art the very draught of blessedness.

How much dost thou raise a soul from earth which uses in its view all things of the vileness of earth.

Thou art poor to look upon, but inwardly thou art full of wealth; thou seemest low, but art exceeding high; thou art that which makest men live a life divine here below.

Give me, O Lord, Thou greatest Goodness, a good portion of this heavenly happiness and true peace, that the world, sensual as it is, is neither capable of understanding nor receiving.

How few are the souls which are willing to forget themselves, to free their hearts from their own affections, their own desires, their own satisfactions, their own love and judgments! That are willing to be led by the highway of self denial and the internal way! That are willing to be annihilated, dying to themselves and their senses.

THE END.

Copyright © 2020 / Alicia Éditions
Credits: Canva
All rights reserved

www.ingramcontent.com/pod-product-compliance
Lightning Source LLC
LaVergne TN
LVHW040157080526
838202LV00042B/3206